STRAIGHT FORWARD

Math Series

MASTERY TESTS

by S. Harold Collins

Book cover design by Kathy Kifer

Published by:
Garlic Press
605 Powers St.
Eugene, OR 97402

ISBN 0-931993-44-X
Order Number GP-044

www.garlicpress.com

To Parents and Teachers and Students,

The Straight Forward Math Series has been designed for parents, teachers and students. The series is a straightforward way to teach basic mathematical operations.

These **Mastery Tests** provide testing, practice, and assessment of <u>addition</u>, <u>subtraction</u>, <u>multiplication</u>, and <u>division</u> skills. Use these steps to mastery:

- **Basic Facts**
  Four sheets are provided for each operation: 4 addition, 4 subtraction, 4 multiplication, and 4 division.

  The first two sheets arrange facts diagonally—see Answers pages 29-32 to see this diagonal arrangement.

  This diagonal arrangement will accent which facts prove difficult to a student. Note how the diagonals are labeled.

  The second two sheets present problems with missing parts. These missing parts require different problem solving skills. Not just regular sums or differences or products or quotients are required for these problems. Most often a problem provides an answer and asks what is needed to arrive at the given answer.

- **Advanced Skills**
  Two sheets are provided for each operation.

  The first sheet is arranged by skills. Note the horizontal listings of skills —see Answers pages 33-34.

  The second sheet provides problems that also have missing parts–like the Basic Facts. The solution to these missing parts is more sophisticated.

- **Assessment Tests**
  The Assessment Tests are the measuring tools to find out what has actually been mastered.

  Four assessment Tests are provided, one for each mathematical operation. Each test is arranged from simple to complex skills—see Answers page 35.

These Mastery Tests have been designed as rigorous exercises which group skills and identify a student's level of mastery. This book can be used along with other books in the Straight Forward Math Series—see other offerings.

The administrator of these tests must also be rigorous. Set standards to progress from sheet to sheet, operation to operation.

Contents

Basic Addition

0 + 9	9 + 8	6 + 7	5 + 4	1 + 3	0 + 2	2 + 1	9 + 0	3 + 0	5 +10
9 + 6	1 + 9	7 + 8	3 + 7	9 + 4	4 + 3	5 + 2	4 + 1	8 + 0	1 + 0
4 + 5	8 + 6	2 + 9	6 + 8	1 + 7	4 + 4	5 + 3	3 + 2	8 + 1	7 + 0
10 + 4	2 + 5	7 + 6	3 + 9	5 + 8	8 + 7	7 + 4	6 + 3	6 + 2	3 + 1
0 + 0	2 + 4	9 + 5	10 + 6	4 + 9	4 + 8	2 + 7	8 + 4	2 + 3	7 + 2
8 + 8	3 + 3	8 + 4	6 + 5	4 + 6	5 + 9	3 + 8	9 + 7	5 + 4	8 + 3
7 + 3	1 + 1	6 + 6	7 + 4	3 + 5	3 + 6	6 + 9	2 + 8	10 + 7	2 + 4
8 + 2	5 + 3	2 + 2	9 + 9	3 + 4	8 + 5	2 + 6	7 + 9	1 + 8	5 + 7
0 +10	9 + 2	10 + 3	5 + 5	10 +10	1 + 4	1 + 5	1 + 6	8 + 9	0 + 8
9 +10	8 +10	10 + 2	0 + 3	4 + 4	7 + 7	0 + 4	7 + 5	0 + 6	9 + 9

Basic Addition

4 + 5 =	3 + 2 =	2 + 6 =	1 + 6 =	0 + 8 =
5 + 6 =	4 + 4 =	3 + 9 =	2 + 7 =	1 + 5 =
6 + 1 =	5 + 7 =	4 + 3 =	3 + 8 =	2 + 8 =
7 + 3 =	6 + 2 =	5 + 8 =	4 + 2 =	3 + 7 =
8 + 8 =	7 + 4 =	6 + 3 =	5 + 9 =	4 + 1 =
9 + 9 =	8 + 9 =	7 + 5 =	6 + 4 =	5 + 5 =
10 + 1 =	9 + 8 =	8 + 1 =	7 + 6 =	6 + 5 =
9 + 5 =	10 + 3 =	9 + 6 =	8 + 2 =	7 + 7 =
8 + 4 =	9 + 9 =	10 + 2 =	9 + 4 =	8 + 3 =
10 + 6 =	8 + 9 =	9 + 8 =	10 + 5 =	9 + 2 =
9 + 9 =	10 + 7 =	8 + 8 =	9 + 1 =	10 + 4 =
8 + 4 =	9 + 7 =	10 + 8 =	8 + 6 =	9 + 5 =
7 + 7 =	8 + 5 =	9 + 5 =	10 + 9 =	8 + 2 =
6 + 6 =	7 + 8 =	8 + 6 =	9 + 3 =	10 + 10 =
5 + 5 =	6 + 9 =	7 + 9 =	8 + 7 =	9 + 1 =
4 + 6 =	5 + 4 =	6 + 8 =	7 + 1 =	8 + 8 =
3 + 3 =	4 + 7 =	5 + 3 =	6 + 7 =	7 + 2 =
2 + 6 =	3 + 4 =	4 + 8 =	5 + 2 =	6 + 6 =
1 + 3 =	2 + 3 =	3 + 5 =	4 + 9 =	5 + 1 =
0 + 6 =	1 + 4 =	2 + 9 =	3 + 9 =	4 + 5 =

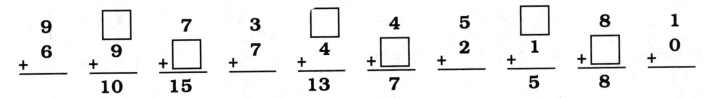

Basic Addition

9 + 6 = ___	□ + 9 = 10	7 + □ = 15	3 + 7 = ___	□ + 4 = 13	4 + □ = 7	5 + 2 = ___	□ + 1 = 5	8 + □ = 8	1 + 0 = ___
□ + 5 = 9	8 + □ = 14	2 + 9 = ___	□ + 8 = 14	1 + □ = 8	4 + 4 = ___	□ + 3 = 8	3 + □ = 5	8 + 1 = ___	□ + 0 = 7
10 + □ = 14	2 + 5 = ___	□ + 6 = 13	3 + □ = 12	5 + 8 = ___	□ + 7 = 15	7 + □ = 11	6 + 3 = ___	□ + 2 = 8	3 + □ = 4
0 + 0 = ___	□ + 4 = 6	9 + □ = 14	10 + 6 = ___	□ + 9 = 13	4 + □ = 12	2 + 7 = ___	□ + 4 = 12	2 + □ = 5	7 + 2 = ___
□ + 8 = 16	3 + □ = 6	8 + 4 = ___	□ + 5 = 11	4 + □ = 10	5 + 9 = ___	□ + 8 = 11	9 + □ = 16	5 + 4 = ___	□ + 3 = 11
7 + □ = 19	1 + 1 = ___	□ + 6 = 12	7 + □ = 11	3 + 5 = ___	□ + 6 = 9	6 + □ = 15	2 + 8 = ___	□ + 7 = 17	2 + □ = 6
8 + 2 = ___	□ + 3 = 8	2 + □ = 4	9 + 9 = ___	□ + 4 = 7	8 + □ = 13	2 + 6 = ___	□ + 9 = 16	1 + □ = 9	5 + 7 = ___
□ + 10 = 10	9 + □ = 11	10 + 3 = ___	□ + 5 = 10	10 + □ = 20	1 + 4 = ___	□ + 5 = 16	1 + □ = 17	8 + 9 = ___	□ + 8 = 8

Basic Addition

5 + 6 =	□ + 4 = 8	3 + □ = 12	2 + 7 =	□ + 5 = 6
6 + □ = 7	5 + 7 =	□ + 3 = 7	3 + □ = 11	2 + 8 =
□ + 3 = 10	6 + □ = 8	5 + 8 =	□ + 2 = 6	3 + □ = 10
8 + 8 =	□ + 4 = 11	6 + □ = 9	5 + 9 =	□ + 1 = 5
9 + □ = 17	8 + 9 =	□ + 5 = 12	6 + □ = 10	5 + 5 =
□ + 1 = 11	9 + □ = 19	8 + 1 =	□ + 6 = 13	6 + □ = 11
9 + 5 =	□ + 3 = 13	9 + □ = 15	8 + 2 =	□ + 7 = 14
8 + □ = 12	9 + 9 =	□ + 2 = 12	9 + □ = 13	8 + 3 =
□ + 6 = 16	8 + □ = 17	9 + 8 =	□ + 5 = 15	9 + □ = 11
9 + 9 =	□ + 7 = 17	8 + □ = 16	9 + 1 =	□ + 4 = 14
8 + □ = 12	9 + 7 =	□ + 8 = 18	8 + □ = 14	9 + 5 =
□ + 7 = 14	8 + □ = 13	9 + 5 =	□ + 9 = 19	8 + □ = 10
6 + 6 =	□ + 8 = 15	8 + □ = 14	9 + 3 =	□ +10 = 20
5 + □ = 10	6 + 9 =	□ + 9 = 16	8 + □ = 15	9 + 1 =
□ + 6 = 13	5 + □ = 9	6 + 8 =	□ + 1 = 8	8 + □ = 16
3 + 3 =	□ + 6 = 10	5 + □ = 8	6 + 7 =	□ + 2 = 16
5 + □ = 11	3 + 4 =	□ + 8 = 12	5 + □ = 7	6 + 6 =

Basic Subtraction

16 - 9	10 - 8	9 - 7	8 - 4	6 - 3	6 - 2	4 - 1	0 - 0	5 - 0	8 - 0
14 - 6	11 - 9	9 - 8	11 - 7	9 - 4	7 - 3	8 - 2	5 - 1	1 - 0	6 - 0
5 - 5	15 - 6	12 - 9	17 - 8	12 - 7	10 - 4	8 - 3	7 - 2	6 - 1	2 - 0
15 - 7	6 - 5	14 - 6	13 - 9	16 - 8	13 - 7	11 - 4	9 - 3	9 - 2	7 - 1
18 - 8	13 - 7	7 - 5	13 - 6	14 - 9	15 - 8	14 - 7	12 - 4	11 - 3	10 - 2
4 - 4	14 - 8	14 - 7	8 - 5	12 - 6	15 - 9	14 - 8	15 - 7	13 - 4	12 - 3
13 - 3	5 - 4	15 - 8	15 - 7	9 - 5	11 - 6	16 - 9	13 - 8	16 - 7	14 - 4
2 - 2	4 - 3	6 - 4	16 - 8	16 - 7	14 - 5	10 - 6	17 - 9	12 - 8	17 - 7
13 - 10	3 - 2	5 - 3	7 - 4	17 - 8	7 - 7	13 - 5	9 - 6	18 - 9	11 - 8
11 - 10	17 - 10	4 - 2	6 - 3	8 - 4	9 - 8	8 - 7	12 - 5	8 - 6	19 - 9

Basic Subtraction

5 - 4 =	7 - 3 =	6 - 2 =	6 - 1 =	10 - 10 =
6 - 5 =	4 - 4 =	9 - 3 =	7 - 2 =	5 - 1 =
9 - 6 =	7 - 5 =	5 - 4 =	8 - 3 =	8 - 2 =
10 - 7 =	8 - 6 =	9 - 5 =	6 - 4 =	7 - 3 =
8 - 8 =	9 - 7 =	9 - 6 =	9 - 5 =	8 - 4 =
10 - 9 =	10 - 8 =	8 - 7 =	9 - 6 =	5 - 5 =
9 - 5 =	9 - 9 =	8 - 8 =	9 - 7 =	10 - 6 =
7 - 0 =	8 - 5 =	10 - 9 =	9 - 8 =	7 - 7 =
9 - 3 =	6 - 0 =	7 - 5 =	9 - 9 =	9 - 8 =
5 - 4 =	8 - 3 =	5 - 0 =	6 - 5 =	10 - 9 =
6 - 5 =	6 - 4 =	7 - 3 =	4 - 0 =	5 - 5 =
7 - 6 =	7 - 5 =	7 - 4 =	6 - 3 =	3 - 0 =
6 - 5 =	8 - 6 =	8 - 5 =	8 - 4 =	5 - 3 =
4 - 3 =	7 - 5 =	9 - 6 =	9 - 5 =	9 - 4 =
6 - 4 =	5 - 3 =	8 - 5 =	10 - 6 =	10 - 5 =
4 - 2 =	7 - 4 =	6 - 3 =	9 - 5 =	8 - 6 =
7 - 3 =	5 - 2 =	8 - 4 =	7 - 3 =	10 - 5 =
8 - 4 =	8 - 3 =	6 - 2 =	9 - 4 =	8 - 3 =
10 - 10 =	6 - 4 =	6 - 3 =	7 - 2 =	10 - 4 =
9 - 5 =	10 - 10 =	5 - 4 =	4 - 3 =	8 - 2 =

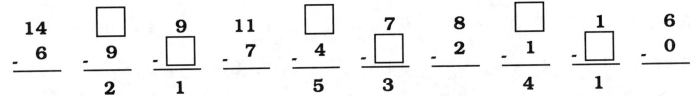

Basic Subtraction

14 − 6 =	□ − 9 = 2	9 − □ = 1	11 − 7 =	□ − 4 = 5	7 − □ = 3	8 − 2 =	□ − 1 = 4	1 − □ = 1	6 − 0 =
□ − 5 = 0	15 − □ = 9	12 − 9 =	□ − 8 = 9	12 − □ = 5	10 − 4 =	□ − 3 = 5	7 − □ = 5	6 − 1 =	□ − 0 = 2
15 − □ = 8	6 − 5 =	□ − 6 = 8	13 − □ = 4	16 − 8 =	□ − 7 = 6	11 − □ = 7	9 − 3 =	□ − 2 = 7	7 − □ = 6
18 − 8 =	□ − 7 = 6	7 − □ = 2	13 − 6 =	□ − 9 = 5	15 − □ = 7	14 − 7 =	□ − 4 = 8	11 − □ = 8	10 − 2 =
□ − 4 = 8	14 − □ = 6	14 − 7 =	□ − 5 = 3	12 − □ = 6	15 − 9 =	□ − 8 = 6	15 − □ = 8	13 − 4 =	□ − 3 = 9
13 − □ = 10	5 − 4 =	□ − 8 = 7	15 − □ = 8	9 − 5 =	□ − 6 = 5	16 − □ = 7	13 − 8 =	□ − 7 = 9	14 − □ = 10
2 − 2 =	□ − 3 = 1	6 − □ = 2	16 − 8 =	□ − 7 = 9	14 − □ = 9	10 − 6 =	□ − 9 = 8	12 − □ = 4	17 − 7 =
□ − 10 = 3	3 − □ = 1	5 − 3 =	□ − 4 = 3	17 − □ = 9	7 − 7 =	□ − 5 = 8	9 − □ = 3	18 − 9 =	□ − 8 = 3

Basic Subtraction

5 - 4 =	□ - 3 = 4	6 - □ = 4	6 - 1 =	□ - 10 = 0
6 - □ = 1	4 - 4 =	□ - 3 = 6	7 - □ = 5	5 - 1 =
□ - 6 = 3	7 - □ = 2	5 - 4 =	□ - 3 = 5	8 - □ = 6
10 - 7 =	□ - 6 = 2	9 - □ = 4	6 - 4 =	□ - 3 = 4
8 - □ = 0	9 - 7 =	□ - 6 = 3	9 - □ = 4	8 - 4 =
□ - 9 = 1	10 - □ = 2	8 - 7 =	□ - 6 = 3	5 - □ = 0
9 - 5 =	□ - 9 = 1	8 - □ = 0	9 - 7 =	□ - 6 = 4
7 - □ = 7	8 - 5 =	□ - 9 = 1	9 - □ = 1	7 - 7 =
□ - 3 = 6	6 - □ = 6	7 - 5 =	□ - 9 = 1	9 - □ = 1
5 - 4 =	□ - 3 = 5	5 - □ = 2	6 - 5 =	□ - 9 = 1
6 - □ = 6	6 - 4 =	□ - 3 = 4	4 - □ = 4	5 - 5 =
□ - 6 = 1	7 - □ = 2	7 - 4 =	□ - 3 = 3	3 - □ = 3
6 - 5 =	□ - 6 = 2	8 - □ = 3	8 - 4 =	□ - 3 = 2
5 - □ = 2	7 - 5 =	□ - 6 = 3	9 - □ = 4	9 - 4 =
□ - 4 = 2	5 - □ = 2	8 - 5 =	□ - 6 = 4	10 - □ = 5
4 - 2 =	□ - 4 = 3	6 - □ = 3	9 - 5 =	□ - 6 = 2
7 - □ = 4	5 - 2 =	□ - 4 = 4	7 - □ = 4	10 - 5 =

Basic Multiplication

9	5	2	6	9	5	3	3	7	8
x 9	x 8	x 7	x 5	x 6	x 2	x 1	x 0	x 0	x10
9	1	8	9	3	7	8	2	5	8
x 3	x 9	x 8	x 7	x 5	x 6	x 2	x 1	x 0	x 0
3	8	2	0	3	7	3	7	5	6
x 4	x 3	x 9	x 8	x 7	x 5	x 6	x 2	x 1	x 0
9	5	7	3	3	8	9	5	6	4
x 2	x 4	x 3	x 9	x 8	x 7	x 5	x 6	x 2	x 1
2	4	2	6	4	7	4	4	8	9
x 2	x 2	x 4	x 3	x 9	x 8	x 7	x 5	x 6	x 2
8	3	8	4	5	5	4	5	8	4
x 8	x 3	x 2	x 4	x 3	x 9	x 8	x 7	x 5	x 6
9	1	7	3	9	4	6	4	6	5
x 1	x 1	x 7	x 2	x 4	x 3	x 9	x 8	x 7	x 5
0	6	5	6	0	7	3	7	6	7
x10	x 1	x 5	x 6	x 2	x 4	x 3	x 9	x 8	x 7
2	6	7	9	0	6	8	2	8	9
x10	x10	x 1	x 9	x 0	x 2	x 4	x 3	x 9	x 8
5	7	9	8	4	5	7	6	1	9
x10	x10	x10	x 1	x 4	x 5	x 2	x 4	x 3	x 9

Basic Multiplication

4 x 5 =	3 x 2 =	2 x 6 =	1 x 6 =	0 x 8 =
5 x 6 =	4 x 4 =	3 x 9 =	2 x 7 =	1 x 5 =
6 x 1 =	5 x 7 =	4 x 3 =	3 x 8 =	2 x 8 =
7 x 3 =	6 x 2 =	5 x 8 =	4 x 2 =	3 x 7 =
8 x 8 =	7 x 4 =	6 x 3 =	5 x 9 =	4 x 1 =
9 x 9 =	8 x 9 =	7 x 5 =	6 x 4 =	5 x 5 =
10 x 1 =	9 x 8 =	8 x 1 =	7 x 6 =	6 x 5 =
9 x 5 =	10 x 3 =	9 x 6 =	8 x 2 =	7 x 7 =
8 x 4 =	9 x 9 =	10 x 2 =	9 x 4 =	8 x 3 =
10 x 6 =	8 x 9 =	9 x 8 =	10 x 5 =	9 x 2 =
9 x 9 =	10 x 7 =	8 x 8 =	9 x 1 =	10 x 4 =
8 x 4 =	9 x 7 =	10 x 8 =	8 x 6 =	9 x 5 =
7 x 7 =	8 x 5 =	9 x 5 =	10 x 9 =	8 x 2 =
6 x 6 =	7 x 8 =	8 x 6 =	9 x 3 =	10 x 10 =
5 x 5 =	6 x 9 =	7 x 9 =	8 x 7 =	9 x 1 =
4 x 6 =	5 x 4 =	6 x 8 =	7 x 1 =	8 x 8 =
3 x 3 =	4 x 6 =	5 x 3 =	6 x 7 =	7 x 2 =
2 x 6 =	3 x 4 =	4 x 8 =	5 x 2 =	6 x 6 =
1 x 3 =	2 x 3 =	3 x 5 =	4 x 9 =	5 x 1 =
0 x 6 =	1 x 4 =	2 x 9 =	3 x 9 =	4 x 5 =

Basic Multiplication

9	□	8	9	□	7	8	□	5	8
x 3	x 9	x □	x 7	x 5	x □	x 2	x 1	x □	x 0
	9	64		15	7		2	0	
□	8	2	□	3	7	□	7	5	□
x 4	x □	x 9	x 8	x □	x 5	x 6	x □	x 1	x 0
12	24		0	21		18	14		0
9	5	□	3	3	□	9	5	□	4
x □	x 4	x 3	x □	x 8	x 7	x □	x 6	x 2	x □
18		21	27		56	45		12	4
2	□	2	6	□	7	4	□	8	9
x 2	x 2	x □	x 3	x 9	x □	x 7	x 5	x □	x 2
	8	8		36	56		20	48	
□	3	8	□	5	5	□	5	8	□
x 8	x □	x 2	x 4	x □	x 9	x 8	x □	x 5	x 6
64	9		16	15		32	35		24
9	1	□	3	9	□	6	4	□	4
x □	x 1	x 7	x □	x 4	x 3	x □	x 8	x 7	x □
9		49	6		12	54		42	24
0	□	5	6	□	7	3	□	6	7
x 10	x 1	x □	x 6	x 2	x □	x 3	x 9	x □	x 7
	6	25		0	28		63	48	
□	6	7	□	0	6	□	2	8	□
x 10	x □	x 1	x 9	x □	x 2	x 4	x □	x 9	x 8
20	60		81	0		32	6		72

Basic Multiplication

5 x 6 =	□ x 4 = 16	3 x □ = 27	2 x 7 =	□ x 5 = 5
6 x □ = 6	5 x 7 =	□ x 3 = 12	3 x □ = 24	2 x 8 =
□ x 3 = 21	6 x □ = 12	5 x 8 =	□ x 2 = 10	3 x □ = 21
8 x 8 =	□ x 4 = 14	6 x □ = 18	5 x 9 =	□ x 1 = 4
9 x □ = 81	8 x 9 =	□ x 5 = 35	6 x □ = 24	5 x 5 =
□ x 1 = 10	9 x □ = 72	8 x 1 =	□ x 6 = 42	6 x □ = 30
9 x 5 =	□ x 3 = 30	9 x □ = 54	8 x 2 =	□ x 7 = 49
8 x □ = 32	9 x 9 =	□ x 2 = 20	9 x □ = 36	8 x 3 =
□ x 6 = 60	8 x □ = 72	9 x 8 =	□ x 5 = 50	9 x □ = 18
9 x 9 =	□ x 7 = 70	8 x □ = 64	9 x 1 =	□ x 4 = 40
8 x □ = 32	9 x 7 =	□ x 8 = 80	8 x □ = 48	9 x 5 =
□ x 7 = 49	8 x □ = 40	9 x 5 =	□ x 9 = 90	8 x □ = 16
6 x 6 =	□ x 8 = 56	8 x □ = 56	9 x 3 =	□ x 10 = 100
5 x □ = 25	6 x 9 =	□ x 9 = 63	8 x □ = 56	9 x 1 =
□ x 6 = 42	5 x □ = 20	6 x 8 =	□ x 1 = 7	8 x □ = 64
3 x 3 =	□ x 6 = 24	5 x □ = 15	6 x 7 =	□ x 2 = 14
5 x □ = 30	3 x 4 =	□ x 8 = 32	5 x □ = 10	6 x 6 =

Basic Division

9)18	8)16	7)7	6)60	5)20	4)16	5)5	6)18	7)28	10)100
3)12	9)54	8)48	7)35	6)12	5)30	4)28	5)10	6)36	7)21
4)8	3)3	9)72	8)72	7)14	6)54	5)45	4)20	5)50	6)48
2)6	4)12	3)9	9)27	8)64	7)63	6)30	5)15	4)36	5)40
1)3	2)4	4)40	3)30	9)81	8)32	7)70	6)48	5)35	4)24
3)27	1)4	2)2	4)32	3)15	9)36	8)0	7)42	6)24	5)10
8)8	3)18	1)7	2)8	4)12	3)27	9)18	8)40	7)56	6)42
2)18	8)56	3)30	1)5	2)10	4)36	3)18	9)9	8)80	7)49
10)60	2)20	8)72	3)21	1)6	2)16	4)24	3)21	9)18	8)24
10)80	10)30	2)0	8)48	3)0	1)8	2)12	4)28	3)9	9)90

Basic Division

$4 \div 4 =$	$12 \div 3 =$	$6 \div 2 =$	$6 \div 1 =$	$8 \div 1 =$
$25 \div 5 =$	$8 \div 4 =$	$9 \div 3 =$	$4 \div 2 =$	$5 \div 1 =$
$30 \div 6 =$	$30 \div 5 =$	$16 \div 4 =$	$6 \div 3 =$	$2 \div 2 =$
$0 \div 7 =$	$24 \div 6 =$	$35 \div 5 =$	$12 \div 4 =$	$27 \div 3 =$
$32 \div 8 =$	$7 \div 7 =$	$18 \div 6 =$	$40 \div 5 =$	$20 \div 4 =$
$45 \div 9 =$	$40 \div 8 =$	$14 \div 7 =$	$12 \div 6 =$	$45 \div 5 =$
$80 \div 10 =$	$36 \div 9 =$	$24 \div 8 =$	$21 \div 7 =$	$6 \div 6 =$
$81 \div 9 =$	$100 \div 10 =$	$9 \div 9 =$	$16 \div 8 =$	$28 \div 7 =$
$72 \div 8 =$	$90 \div 9 =$	$60 \div 10 =$	$18 \div 9 =$	$8 \div 8 =$
$63 \div 7 =$	$8 \div 8 =$	$63 \div 9 =$	$40 \div 10 =$	$27 \div 9 =$
$36 \div 6 =$	$56 \div 7 =$	$56 \div 8 =$	$72 \div 9 =$	$20 \div 10 =$
$20 \div 5 =$	$42 \div 6 =$	$49 \div 7 =$	$64 \div 8 =$	$54 \div 9 =$
$28 \div 4 =$	$15 \div 5 =$	$48 \div 6 =$	$42 \div 7 =$	$48 \div 8 =$
$12 \div 3 =$	$36 \div 4 =$	$10 \div 5 =$	$54 \div 6 =$	$35 \div 7 =$
$24 \div 4 =$	$15 \div 3 =$	$32 \div 4 =$	$50 \div 5 =$	$36 \div 6 =$
$45 \div 5 =$	$28 \div 4 =$	$18 \div 3 =$	$28 \div 4 =$	$0 \div 5 =$
$60 \div 6 =$	$5 \div 5 =$	$32 \div 4 =$	$21 \div 3 =$	$24 \div 4 =$
$6 \div 1 =$	$42 \div 6 =$	$0 \div 5 =$	$40 \div 4 =$	$24 \div 3 =$
$20 \div 2 =$	$2 \div 1 =$	$18 \div 6 =$	$50 \div 5 =$	$36 \div 4 =$
$18 \div 2 =$	$0 \div 2 =$	$10 \div 1 =$	$30 \div 6 =$	$35 \div 5 =$

Basic Division

$3\overline{)12}$ $\overset{6}{\square\overline{)54}}$ $\overset{6}{8\overline{)\square}}$ $7\overline{)35}$ $\overset{2}{\square\overline{)12}}$ $\overset{6}{5\overline{)\square}}$ $4\overline{)28}$ $\overset{2}{\square\overline{)10}}$ $\overset{6}{6\overline{)\square}}$ $7\overline{)21}$

$\overset{2}{\square\overline{)8}}$ $\overset{1}{3\overline{)\square}}$ $9\overline{)72}$ $\overset{9}{\square\overline{)72}}$ $\overset{2}{7\overline{)\square}}$ $6\overline{)54}$ $\overset{9}{\square\overline{)45}}$ $\overset{4}{4\overline{)\square}}$ $5\overline{)50}$ $\overset{8}{\square\overline{)48}}$

$\overset{3}{2\overline{)\square}}$ $4\overline{)12}$ $\overset{3}{\square\overline{)9}}$ $\overset{9}{9\overline{)\square}}$ $8\overline{)64}$ $\overset{9}{\square\overline{)63}}$ $\overset{5}{6\overline{)\square}}$ $5\overline{)15}$ $\overset{9}{\square\overline{)36}}$ $\overset{8}{5\overline{)\square}}$

$1\overline{)3}$ $\overset{2}{\square\overline{)4}}$ $\overset{10}{4\overline{)\square}}$ $3\overline{)30}$ $\overset{9}{\square\overline{)81}}$ $\overset{4}{8\overline{)\square}}$ $7\overline{)70}$ $\overset{8}{\square\overline{)48}}$ $\overset{7}{5\overline{)\square}}$ $4\overline{)24}$

$\overset{9}{\square\overline{)27}}$ $\overset{4}{1\overline{)\square}}$ $2\overline{)2}$ $\overset{8}{\square\overline{)32}}$ $\overset{5}{3\overline{)\square}}$ $9\overline{)36}$ $\overset{0}{\square\overline{)0}}$ $\overset{6}{7\overline{)\square}}$ $6\overline{)24}$ $\overset{2}{\square\overline{)10}}$

$\overset{1}{8\overline{)\square}}$ $3\overline{)18}$ $\overset{7}{\square\overline{)7}}$ $\overset{4}{2\overline{)\square}}$ $4\overline{)12}$ $\overset{9}{\square\overline{)27}}$ $\overset{2}{9\overline{)\square}}$ $8\overline{)40}$ $\overset{8}{\square\overline{)56}}$ $\overset{7}{6\overline{)\square}}$

$2\overline{)18}$ $\overset{7}{\square\overline{)56}}$ $\overset{10}{3\overline{)\square}}$ $1\overline{)5}$ $\overset{5}{\square\overline{)10}}$ $\overset{9}{4\overline{)\square}}$ $3\overline{)18}$ $\overset{1}{\square\overline{)9}}$ $\overset{10}{8\overline{)\square}}$ $7\overline{)49}$

$\overset{6}{\square\overline{)60}}$ $\overset{10}{2\overline{)\square}}$ $8\overline{)72}$ $\overset{7}{\square\overline{)21}}$ $\overset{6}{1\overline{)\square}}$ $2\overline{)16}$ $\overset{6}{\square\overline{)24}}$ $\overset{7}{3\overline{)\square}}$ $9\overline{)18}$ $\overset{3}{\square\overline{)24}}$

Basic Division

25 ÷ 5 =	□ ÷ 4 = 2	9 ÷ □ = 3	4 ÷ 2 =	□ ÷ 1 = 5
30 ÷ □ = 5	30 ÷ 5 =	□ ÷ 4 = 4	6 ÷ □ = 2	2 ÷ 2 =
□ ÷ 0 = 0	24 ÷ □ = 4	35 ÷ 5 =	□ ÷ 4 = 3	27 ÷ □ = 9
32 ÷ 8 =	□ ÷ 7 = 1	18 ÷ □ = 3	40 ÷ 5 =	□ ÷ 4 = 5
45 ÷ □ = 5	40 ÷ 8 =	□ ÷ 7 = 2	12 ÷ □ = 2	45 ÷ 5 =
□ ÷ 10 = 8	36 ÷ □ = 4	24 ÷ 8 =	□ ÷ 7 = 3	6 ÷ □ = 1
81 ÷ 9 =	□ ÷ 10 = 10	9 ÷ □ = 1	16 ÷ 8 =	□ ÷ 7 = 4
72 ÷ □ = 9	90 ÷ 9 =	□ ÷ 10 = 6	18 ÷ □ = 2	8 ÷ 8 =
□ ÷ 7 = 9	8 ÷ □ = 1	63 ÷ 9 =	□ ÷ 10 = 4	27 ÷ □ = 3
36 ÷ 6 =	□ ÷ 7 = 8	56 ÷ □ = 7	72 ÷ 9 =	□ ÷ 10 = 2
20 ÷ □ = 4	42 ÷ 6 =	□ ÷ 7 = 7	64 ÷ □ = 8	54 ÷ 9 =
□ ÷ 4 = 7	15 ÷ □ = 3	48 ÷ 6 =	□ ÷ 7 = 6	48 ÷ □ = 6
12 ÷ 3 =	□ ÷ 4 = 8	10 ÷ □ = 2	54 ÷ 6 =	□ ÷ 7 = 5
24 ÷ □ = 6	15 ÷ 3 =	□ ÷ 4 = 4	50 ÷ □ = 5	36 ÷ 6 =
□ ÷ 5 = 9	28 ÷ □ = 7	18 ÷ 3 =	□ ÷ 4 = 7	40 ÷ □ = 8
45 ÷ 9 =	□ ÷ 5 = 1	32 ÷ □ = 8	21 ÷ 3 =	□ ÷ 4 = 6
6 ÷ □ = 6	60 ÷ 10 =	□ ÷ 5 = 0	40 ÷ □ = 5	24 ÷ 3 =

Advanced Addition

13 + 45	32 + 37	15 + 24	44 + 14	23 + 72	21 22 + 23	35 23 + 11

513 + 64	24 + 603	323 + 56	832 + 32	417 40 + 31	744 32 + 10	525 52 + 11

36 + 29	27 + 34	57 + 23	73 + 18	26 + 86	49 + 65	98 + 88

46 26 + 16	19 50 + 28	53 28 + 15	41 16 + 27	67 66 + 65	85 95 + 55	93 94 + 95

324 + 36	627 + 47	866 + 25	294 + 576	368 + 347	298 + 304

769 + 754	381 + 709	576 + 557	274 + 790	894 + 858	631 + 769

1,492 + 1,986	4,455 + 7,786	42,791 + 23,489	487,692 + 255,508	2,987,465 + 8,978,645

Advanced Addition

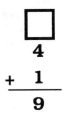

□	2	6	1	□	8	4
4	□	0	2	7	□	9
+ 1	+ 2	+ □	+ 5	+ 2	+ 6	+ □
9	10	9		14	17	19

					□	35
52	□	56	70	□	11	□
+ □	+ 82	+ 43	+ □	+ 24	+ 33	+ 11
76	93		89	48	67	69

			□	523	713	224
□	513	942	40	□	46	132
+ 72	+ □	+ 30	+ 31	+ 23	+ 30	+ □
489	577		488	569		467

□	88	28	□	47	□	18
+ 7	+ 2	+ □	+ 8	+ 6	+ 27	+ □
42		37	52		46	43

				□	19	18
68	□	64	46	28	□	64
+ 54	+ 96	+ □	+ 85	+ 15	+ 18	+ 69
	190	100		90	65	

440	278	□	594	394	□	472
+ 39	+ □	+ 99	+ 186	+ □	+ 239	+ 668
	297	608		969	625	

□	1,327	28,097	□
+ 1,912	+ 9,857	+ □	+ 7,568,705
4,380		39,743	13,116,311

Advanced Subtraction

89	167	882	795	987	768
- 52	- 37	- 631	- 33	- 456	- 432
98	51	92	82	75	73
- 49	- 34	- 28	- 56	- 28	- 26
765	977	372	748	936	814
- 18	- 29	- 67	- 567	- 284	- 373
357	621	971	872	523	743
- 199	- 149	- 565	- 186	- 147	- 265
700	801	670	900	509	403
- 524	- 137	- 485	- 462	- 269	- 148

64,005	9,786	27,142	87,942
- 21,564	- 8,898	- 16,193	- 28,853

Advanced Subtraction

□ − 3 = 74	89 − □ = 83	68 − 22 =	□ − 9 = 20	36 − □ = 22	97 − 43 =
24 − 5 =	□ − 8 = 34	80 − □ = 44	51 − 8 =	□ − 18 = 38	72 − □ = 4
883 − □ = 853	□ − 24 = 723	882 − 631 =	□ − 56 = 109	276 − □ = 238	493 − 27 =
674 − 146 =	813 − □ = 354	□ − 247 = 188	644 − 176 =	657 − □ = 389	□ − 548 = 368
800 − □ = 236	□ − 351 = 559	407 − 239 =	500 − □ = 345	□ − 276 = 544	704 − 306 =

□ − 357 = 3,919	7,842 − □ = 5,856	56,235 − 24,891 =	□ − 65,974 = 18,557

Advanced Multiplication

56 x 5	70 x 6	49 x 9	64 x 8	39 x 7
492 x 4	300 x 5	628 x 6	749 x 9	508 x 8
436 x 58	257 x 40	587 x 39	823 x 75	784 x 96
456 x 329	357 x 400	706 x 405	376 x 284	592 x 438
995 x 897	9,000 x 800	4,873 x 95	5,870 x 674	2,478 x 352

Advanced Multiplication

☐	51	74	☐	90
x 4	x ☐	x 2	x 3	x ☐
128	153		249	720

93	☐	58	68	☐
x 5	x 4	x ☐	x 9	x 5
	308	348		380

☐	568	533	☐	671
x 6	x ☐	x 3	x 9	x ☐
2,442	1,136		5,652	5,368

14	☐	74	57	☐
x 15	x 28	x ☐	x 85	x 40
	1,316	2,664		3,920

☐	298	607	☐	294
x 62	x ☐	x 47	x 500	x ☐
21,390	7,450		150,000	75,264

☐	264	☐	2,894
x 383	x 804	x 42	x ☐
159,711		227,094	538,284

Advanced Division

5)38	6)27	3)81	4)84	5)90
6)76	5)94	8)891	7)882	4)915
29)87	16)93	30)810	42)970	92)999
37)8,658	83)9,960	39)6,000	48)46,261	72)89,496
250)95,500	701)64,549	342)712,044	692)641,950	547)896,721

Advanced Division

2) 15	5 R1 4) ☐	20 ☐) 60	4) 72	14 7) ☐
17 R1 ☐) 86	9) 96	263 2) ☐	84 R1 ☐) 505	8) 549
9 10) ☐	5 R3 ☐) 88	52) 786	36 R20 26) ☐	25 ☐) 925
64) 6,259	330 24) ☐	76) 53,656	357 R17 ☐) 13,583	90) 68,892
60 R522 741) ☐	233) 94,973	198 R54 ☐) 88,560	540) 756,000	251) 176,955

Assessment Test

21	12	32	18	62	41	36
+ 4	+ 7	+ 6	+ 1	+ 5	+ 7	+ 3

23	54	29	16	32	88	79
+ 8	+ 6	+ 7	+ 9	+ 8	+ 6	+ 5

43	59	73	77	94	76	89
+ 87	+ 46	+ 98	+ 35	+ 29	+ 45	+ 88

13	27	36	24	77	56	98
29	28	23	18	77	46	94
+ 17	+ 14	+ 29	+ 17	+ 77	+ 48	+ 19

132	118	207	655	247	534
+ 48	+ 34	+ 64	+ 66	+ 75	+ 86

359	285	174	689	483	545
+ 578	+ 539	+ 508	+ 734	+ 838	+ 669

6,719	132,074	237,601	827,621	987,465
+ 1,299	+ 678,349	+ 948,709	+ 746,587	+ 978,645

Assessment Test

24	30	42	31	62	43	86
- 5	- 6	- 8	- 4	- 8	- 7	- 9
90	51	98	52	92	61	85
- 24	- 15	- 49	- 27	- 39	- 43	- 26
638	522	345	782	276	333	
- 48	- 97	- 56	- 91	- 87	- 82	
250	381	354	836	910	427	
- 125	- 292	- 117	- 268	- 285	- 208	
420	807	870	608	906	700	
- 115	- 174	- 326	- 399	- 207	- 234	
6,002	7,342	15,167	86,723	86,271		
- 2,453	- 1,565	- 12,368	- 47,268	- 79,452		

Assessment Test

63 x 7	75 x 6	39 x 9	59 x 4	48 x 5
678 x 56	243 x 27	493 x 83	389 x 89	642 x 65
213 x 124	397 x 486	258 x 274	998 x 989	548 x 813
100 x 57	949 x 70	700 x 700	405 x 90	564 x 800
4,673 x 53	5,407 x 42	2,894 x 186	6,677 x 549	4,927 x 238

Assessment Test

5) 29	2) 11	7) 58	8) 66	9) 90
4) 63	3) 28	7) 975	4) 867	6) 838
12) 60	21) 96	18) 936	30) 700	42) 970

50) 2,250	29) 2,436	34) 90,930	42) 10,000
308) 46,278	478) 85,900	187) 100,232	540) 756,000

Basic Addition, Page 1.

0 + 9 = 9	9 + 8 = 17	6 + 7 = 13	5 + 4 = 9	1 + 3 = 4	0 + 2 = 2	2 + 1 = 3	9 + 0 = 9	3 + 0 = 3	5 +10 = 15	
9 + 6 = 15	1 + 9 = 10	7 + 8 = 15	3 + 7 = 10	9 + 4 = 13	4 + 3 = 7	5 + 2 = 7	4 + 1 = 5	8 + 0 = 8	1 + 0 = 1	10's
4 + 5 = 9	8 + 6 = 14	2 + 9 = 11	6 + 8 = 14	1 + 7 = 8	4 + 4 = 8	5 + 3 = 8	3 + 2 = 5	8 + 1 = 9	7 + 0 = 7	0's
10 + 4 = 14	2 + 5 = 7	7 + 6 = 13	3 + 9 = 12	5 + 8 = 13	8 + 7 = 15	7 + 4 = 11	6 + 3 = 9	6 + 2 = 8	3 + 1 = 4	0's
0 + 0 = 0	2 + 4 = 6	9 + 5 = 14	10 + 6 = 16	4 + 9 = 13	4 + 8 = 12	2 + 7 = 9	8 + 4 = 12	2 + 3 = 5	7 + 2 = 9	1's
8 + 8 = 16	3 + 3 = 6	8 + 4 = 12	6 + 5 = 11	4 + 6 = 10	5 + 9 = 14	3 + 8 = 11	9 + 7 = 16	5 + 4 = 9	8 + 3 = 11	2's
7 + 3 = 10	1 + 1 = 2	6 + 6 = 12	7 + 4 = 11	3 + 5 = 8	3 + 6 = 9	6 + 9 = 15	2 + 8 = 10	10 + 7 = 17	2 + 4 = 6	3's
8 + 2 = 10	5 + 3 = 8	2 + 2 = 4	9 + 9 = 18	3 + 4 = 7	8 + 5 = 13	2 + 6 = 8	7 + 9 = 16	1 + 8 = 9	5 + 7 = 12	4's
0 +10 = 10	9 + 2 = 11	10 + 3 = 13	5 + 5 = 10	10 +10 = 20	1 + 4 = 5	1 + 5 = 6	1 + 6 = 7	8 + 9 = 17	0 + 8 = 8	7's
9 +10 = 19	8 +10 = 18	10 + 2 = 12	0 + 3 = 3	4 + 4 = 8	7 + 7 = 14	0 + 4 = 4	7 + 5 = 12	0 + 6 = 6	9 + 9 = 18	8's
10's	10's	2's	3's	Doubles		4's	5's	6's	9's	

Basic Addition, Page 2.

4 + 5 = 9	3 + 2 = 5	2 + 6 = 8	1 + 6 = 7	0 + 8 = 8	0's
5 + 6 = 11	4 + 4 = 8	3 + 9 = 12	2 + 7 = 9	1 + 5 = 6	1's
6 + 1 = 7	5 + 7 = 12	4 + 3 = 7	3 + 8 = 11	2 + 8 = 10	2's
7 + 3 = 10	6 + 2 = 8	5 + 8 = 13	4 + 2 = 6	3 + 7 = 10	3's
8 + 8 = 16	7 + 4 = 11	6 + 3 = 9	5 + 9 = 14	4 + 1 = 5	4's
9 + 9 = 18	8 + 9 = 17	7 + 5 = 12	6 + 4 = 10	5 + 5 = 10	5's
10 + 1 = 11	9 + 8 = 17	8 + 1 = 9	7 + 6 = 13	6 + 5 = 11	6's
9 + 5 = 14	10 + 3 = 13	9 + 6 = 15	8 + 2 = 10	7 + 7 = 14	7's
8 + 4 = 12	9 + 9 = 18	10 + 2 = 12	9 + 4 = 13	8 + 3 = 11	8's
10 + 6 = 16	8 + 9 = 17	9 + 8 = 17	10 + 5 = 15	9 + 2 = 11	9's
9 + 9 = 18	10 + 7 = 17	8 + 8 = 16	9 + 1 = 10	10 + 4 = 14	10's
8 + 4 = 12	9 + 7 = 16	10 + 8 = 18	8 + 6 = 14	9 + 5 = 14	9's
7 + 7 = 14	8 + 5 = 13	9 + 5 = 14	10 + 9 = 19	8 + 2 = 10	8's
6 + 6 = 12	7 + 8 = 15	8 + 6 = 14	9 + 3 = 12	10 + 10 = 20	10'
5 + 5 = 10	6 + 9 = 15	7 + 9 = 16	8 + 7 = 15	9 + 1 = 10	9's
4 + 6 = 10	5 + 4 = 9	6 + 8 = 14	7 + 1 = 8	8 + 8 = 16	8's
3 + 3 = 6	4 + 7 = 11	5 + 3 = 8	6 + 7 = 13	7 + 2 = 9	7's
2 + 6 = 8	3 + 4 = 7	4 + 8 = 12	5 + 2 = 7	6 + 6 = 12	6's
1 + 3 = 4	2 + 3 = 5	3 + 5 = 8	4 + 9 = 13	5 + 1 = 6	5's
0 + 6 = 6	1 + 4 = 5	2 + 9 = 11	3 + 9 = 12	4 + 5 = 9	
	0's	1's	2's	3's	4's

Basic Addition, Page 3.

9 + 6 = 15	[1] + 9 = 10	7 + [8] = 15	3 + 7 = 10	[9] + 4 = 13	4 + [3] = 7	5 + 2 = 7	[4] + 1 = 5	8 + [0] = 8	1 + 0 = 1
[4] + 5 = 9	8 + [6] = 14	2 + 9 = 11	[6] + 8 = 14	1 + [7] = 8	4 + 4 = 8	[5] + 3 = 8	3 + [2] = 5	8 + 1 = 9	[7] + 0 = 7
10 + [4] = 14	2 + 5 = 7	[7] + 6 = 13	3 + [9] = 12	5 + 8 = 13	[8] + 7 = 15	7 + [4] = 11	6 + 3 = 9	[6] + 2 = 8	3 + [1] = 4
0 + 0 = 0	[2] + 4 = 6	9 + [5] = 14	10 + 6 = 16	[4] + 9 = 13	4 + [8] = 12	2 + 7 = 9	[8] + 4 = 12	2 + [3] = 5	7 + 2 = 9
[8] + 8 = 16	3 + [3] = 6	8 + 4 = 12	[6] + 5 = 11	4 + [6] = 10	5 + 9 = 14	[3] + 8 = 11	9 + [7] = 16	5 + 4 = 9	[8] + 3 = 11
7 + [12] = 19	1 + 1 = 2	[6] + 6 = 12	7 + [4] = 11	3 + 5 = 8	[3] + 6 = 9	6 + [9] = 15	2 + 8 = 10	[10] + 7 = 17	2 + [4] = 6
8 + 2 = 10	[5] + 3 = 8	2 + [2] = 4	9 + 9 = 18	[3] + 4 = 7	8 + [5] = 13	2 + 6 = 8	[7] + 9 = 16	1 + [8] = 9	5 + 7 = 12
[0] + 10 = 10	9 + [2] = 11	10 + 3 = 13	[5] + 5 = 10	10 + [10] = 20	1 + 4 = 5	[11] + 5 = 16	1 + [16] = 17	8 + 9 = 17	[0] + 8 = 8

Basic Addition, Page 4.

5 + 6 = 11	[4] + 4 = 8	3 + [9] = 12	2 + 7 = 9	[1] + 5 = 6
6 + [1] = 7	5 + 7 = 12	[4] + 3 = 7	3 + [8] = 11	2 + 8 = 10
[7] + 3 = 10	6 + [2] = 8	5 + 8 = 13	[4] + 2 = 6	3 + [7] = 10
8 + 8 = 16	[7] + 4 = 11	6 + [3] = 9	5 + 9 = 14	[4] + 1 = 5
9 + [8] = 17	8 + 9 = 17	[7] + 5 = 12	6 + [4] = 10	5 + 5 = 10
[10] + 1 = 11	9 + [10] = 19	8 + 1 = 9	[7] + 6 = 13	6 + [5] = 11
9 + 5 = 14	[10] + 3 = 13	9 + [6] = 15	8 + 2 = 10	[7] + 7 = 14
8 + [4] = 12	9 + 9 = 18	[10] + 2 = 12	9 + [4] = 13	8 + 3 = 11
[10] + 6 = 16	8 + [9] = 17	9 + 8 = 17	[10] + 5 = 15	9 + [2] = 11
9 + 9 = 18	[10] + 7 = 17	8 + [8] = 16	9 + 1 = 10	[10] + 4 = 14
8 + [4] = 12	9 + 7 = 16	[10] + 8 = 18	8 + [6] = 14	9 + 5 = 14
[7] + 7 = 14	8 + [5] = 13	9 + 5 = 14	[10] + 9 = 19	8 + [2] = 10
6 + 6 = 12	[7] + 8 = 15	8 + [6] = 14	9 + 3 = 12	[10] + 10 = 20
5 + [5] = 10	6 + 9 = 15	[7] + 9 = 16	8 + [7] = 15	9 + 1 = 10
[7] + 6 = 13	5 + [4] = 9	6 + 8 = 14	[7] + 1 = 8	8 + [8] = 16
3 + 3 = 6	[4] + 6 = 10	5 + [3] = 8	6 + 7 = 13	[14] + 2 = 16
5 + [6] = 11	3 + 4 = 7	[4] + 8 = 12	5 + [2] = 7	6 + 6 = 12

Basic Page 5.

16 - 9 = 7	10 - 8 = 2	9 - 7 = 2	8 - 4 = 4	6 - 3 = 3	6 - 2 = 4	4 - 1 = 3	0 - 0 = 0	5 - 0 = 5	8 - 0 = 8	
14 - 6 = 8	11 - 9 = 2	9 - 8 = 1	11 - 7 = 4	9 - 4 = 5	7 - 3 = 4	8 - 2 = 6	5 - 1 = 4	1 - 0 = 1	6 - 0 = 6	0's
5 - 5 = 0	15 - 6 = 9	12 - 9 = 3	17 - 8 = 9	12 - 7 = 5	10 - 4 = 6	8 - 3 = 5	7 - 2 = 5	6 - 1 = 5	2 - 0 = 2	0's
15 - 7 = 8	6 - 5 = 1	14 - 6 = 8	13 - 9 = 4	16 - 8 = 8	13 - 7 = 6	11 - 4 = 7	9 - 3 = 6	9 - 2 = 7	7 - 1 = 6	0's
18 - 8 = 10	13 - 7 = 6	7 - 5 = 2	13 - 6 = 7	14 - 9 = 5	15 - 8 = 7	14 - 7 = 7	12 - 4 = 8	11 - 3 = 8	10 - 2 = 8	1's
4 - 4 = 0	14 - 8 = 6	14 - 7 = 7	8 - 5 = 3	12 - 6 = 6	15 - 9 = 6	14 - 8 = 6	15 - 7 = 8	13 - 4 = 9	12 - 3 = 9	2's
13 - 3 = 10	5 - 4 = 1	15 - 8 = 7	15 - 7 = 8	9 - 5 = 4	11 - 6 = 5	16 - 9 = 7	13 - 8 = 5	16 - 7 = 9	14 - 4 = 10	3's
2 - 2 = 0	4 - 3 = 1	6 - 4 = 2	16 - 8 = 8	16 - 7 = 9	14 - 5 = 9	10 - 6 = 4	17 - 9 = 8	12 - 8 = 4	17 - 7 = 10	4's
13 - 10 = 3	3 - 2 = 1	5 - 3 = 2	7 - 4 = 3	17 - 8 = 9	7 - 7 = 0	13 - 5 = 8	9 - 6 = 3	18 - 9 = 9	11 - 8 = 3	7's
11 - 10 = 1	17 - 10 = 7	4 - 2 = 2	6 - 3 = 3	8 - 4 = 4	9 - 8 = 1	8 - 7 = 1	12 - 5 = 7	8 - 6 = 2	19 - 9 = 10	8's
10's	10's	2's	3's	4's	8's	7's	5's	6's	9's	

Basic Subtraction, Page 6.

5 - 4 = 1	7 - 3 = 4	6 - 2 = 4	6 - 1 = 5	10 - 10 = 0	10's
6 - 5 = 1	4 - 4 = 0	9 - 3 = 6	7 - 2 = 5	5 - 1 = 4	1's
9 - 6 = 3	7 - 5 = 2	5 - 4 = 1	8 - 3 = 5	8 - 2 = 6	2's
10 - 7 = 3	8 - 6 = 2	9 - 5 = 4	6 - 4 = 2	7 - 3 = 4	3's
8 - 8 = 0	9 - 7 = 2	9 - 6 = 3	9 - 5 = 4	8 - 4 = 4	4's
10 - 9 = 1	10 - 8 = 2	8 - 7 = 1	9 - 6 = 3	5 - 5 = 0	5's
9 - 5 = 4	9 - 9 = 0	8 - 8 = 0	9 - 7 = 2	10 - 6 = 4	6's
7 - 0 = 7	8 - 5 = 3	10 - 9 = 1	9 - 8 = 1	7 - 7 = 0	7's
9 - 3 = 6	6 - 0 = 6	7 - 5 = 2	9 - 9 = 0	9 - 8 = 1	8's
5 - 4 = 1	8 - 3 = 5	5 - 0 = 5	6 - 5 = 1	10 - 9 = 1	9's
6 - 5 = 1	6 - 4 = 2	7 - 3 = 4	4 - 0 = 4	5 - 5 = 0	5's
7 - 6 = 1	7 - 5 = 2	7 - 4 = 3	6 - 3 = 3	3 - 0 = 3	0's
6 - 5 = 1	8 - 6 = 2	8 - 5 = 3	8 - 4 = 4	5 - 3 = 2	3's
4 - 3 = 1	7 - 5 = 2	9 - 6 = 3	9 - 5 = 4	9 - 4 = 5	4's
6 - 4 = 2	5 - 3 = 2	8 - 5 = 3	10 - 6 = 4	10 - 5 = 5	5's
4 - 2 = 2	7 - 4 = 3	6 - 3 = 3	9 - 5 = 4	8 - 6 = 2	6's
7 - 3 = 4	5 - 2 = 3	8 - 4 = 4	7 - 3 = 4	10 - 5 = 5	5's
8 - 4 = 4	8 - 3 = 5	6 - 2 = 4	9 - 4 = 5	8 - 3 = 5	3's
10 - 10 = 0	6 - 4 = 2	6 - 3 = 3	7 - 2 = 5	10 - 4 = 6	4's
9 - 5 = 4	10 - 10 = 0	5 - 4 = 1	4 - 3 = 1	8 - 2 = 6	
5's	10's	4's	3's	2's	

Basic Subtraction, Page 7.

14 - 6 = 8	[11] - 9 = 2	9 - [8] = 1	11 - 7 = 4	[9] - 4 = 5	7 - [4] = 3	8 - 2 = 6	[5] - 1 = 4	1 - [0] = 1	6 - 0 = 6
[5] - 5 = 0	15 - [6] = 9	12 - 9 = 3	[17] - 8 = 9	12 - [7] = 5	10 - 4 = 6	[8] - 3 = 5	7 - [2] = 5	6 - 1 = 5	[2] - 0 = 2
15 - [7] = 8	6 - 5 = 1	[14] - 6 = 8	13 - [9] = 4	16 - 8 = 8	[13] - 7 = 6	11 - [4] = 7	9 - 3 = 6	[9] - 2 = 7	7 - [1] = 6
18 - 8 = 0	[13] - 7 = 6	7 - [5] = 2	13 - 6 = 7	[14] - 9 = 5	15 - [8] = 7	14 - 7 = 7	[12] - 4 = 8	11 - [3] = 8	10 - 2 = 8
[12] - 4 = 8	14 - [8] = 6	14 - 7 = 7	[8] - 5 = 3	12 - [6] = 6	15 - 9 = 6	[14] - 8 = 6	15 - [7] = 8	13 - 4 = 9	[12] - 3 = 9
13 - [3] = 10	5 - 4 = 1	[15] - 8 = 7	15 - [7] = 8	9 - 5 = 4	[11] - 6 = 5	16 - [9] = 7	13 - 8 = 5	[16] - 7 = 9	14 - [4] = 10
2 - 2 = 0	[4] - 3 = 1	6 - [4] = 2	16 - 8 = 8	[16] - 7 = 9	14 - [5] = 9	10 - 6 = 4	[17] - 9 = 8	12 - [8] = 4	17 - 7 = 10
[13] - 10 = 3	3 - [2] = 1	5 - 3 = 2	[7] - 4 = 3	17 - [8] = 9	7 - 7 = 0	[13] - 5 = 8	9 - [6] = 3	18 - 9 = 9	[11] - 8 = 3

Basic Subtraction, Page 8.

5 - 4 = 1	[7] - 3 = 4	6 - [2] = 4	6 - 1 = 5	[10] - 10 = 0
6 - [5] = 1	4 - 4 = 0	[9] - 3 = 6	7 - [2] = 5	5 - 1 = 4
[9] - 6 = 3	7 - [5] = 2	5 - 4 = 1	[8] - 3 = 5	8 - [2] = 6
10 - 7 = 3	[8] - 6 = 2	9 - [5] = 4	6 - 4 = 2	[7] - 3 = 4
8 - [8] = 0	9 - 7 = 2	[9] - 6 = 3	9 - [5] = 4	8 - 4 = 4
[10] - 9 = 1	10 - [8] = 2	8 - 7 = 1	[9] - 6 = 3	5 - [5] = 0
9 - 5 = 4	[10] - 9 = 1	8 - [8] = 0	9 - 7 = 2	[10] - 6 = 4
7 - [0] = 7	8 - 5 = 3	[10] - 9 = 1	9 - [8] = 1	7 - 7 = 0
[9] - 3 = 6	6 - [0] = 6	7 - 5 = 2	[10] - 9 = 1	9 - [8] = 1
5 - 4 = 1	[8] - 3 = 5	5 - [3] = 2	6 - 5 = 1	[10] - 9 = 1
6 - [0] = 6	6 - 4 = 2	[7] - 3 = 4	4 - [0] = 4	5 - 5 = 0
[7] - 6 = 1	7 - [5] = 2	7 - 4 = 3	[6] - 3 = 3	3 - [0] = 3
6 - 5 = 1	[8] - 6 = 2	8 - [5] = 3	8 - 4 = 4	[5] - 3 = 2
5 - [3] = 2	7 - 5 = 2	[9] - 6 = 3	9 - [5] = 4	9 - 4 = 5
[6] - 4 = 2	5 - [3] = 2	8 - 5 = 3	[10] - 6 = 4	10 - [5] = 5
4 - 2 = 2	[7] - 4 = 3	6 - [3] = 3	9 - 5 = 4	[8] - 6 = 2
7 - [3] = 4	5 - 2 = 3	[8] - 4 = 4	7 - [3] = 4	10 - 5 = 5

Basic Multiplication, Page 9.

9 x 9 = 81	5 x 8 = 40	2 x 7 = 14	6 x 5 = 30	9 x 6 = 54	5 x 2 = 10	3 x 1 = 3	3 x 0 = 0	7 x 0 = 0	8 x10 = 80
9 x 3 = 27	1 x 9 = 9	8 x 8 = 64	9 x 7 = 63	3 x 5 = 15	7 x 6 = 42	8 x 2 = 16	2 x 1 = 2	5 x 0 = 0	8 x 0 = 0
3 x 4 = 12	8 x 3 = 24	2 x 9 = 18	0 x 8 = 0	3 x 7 = 21	7 x 5 = 35	3 x 6 = 18	7 x 2 = 14	5 x 1 = 5	6 x 0 = 0
9 x 2 = 18	5 x 4 = 20	7 x 3 = 21	3 x 9 = 27	3 x 8 = 24	8 x 7 = 56	9 x 5 = 45	5 x 6 = 30	6 x 2 = 12	4 x 1 = 4
2 x 2 = 4	4 x 2 = 8	2 x 4 = 8	6 x 3 = 18	4 x 9 = 36	7 x 8 = 56	4 x 7 = 28	4 x 5 = 20	8 x 6 = 48	9 x 2 = 18
8 x 8 = 64	3 x 3 = 9	8 x 2 = 16	4 x 4 = 16	5 x 3 = 15	5 x 9 = 45	4 x 8 = 32	5 x 7 = 35	8 x 5 = 40	4 x 6 = 24
9 x 1 = 9	1 x 1 = 1	7 x 7 = 49	3 x 2 = 6	9 x 4 = 36	4 x 3 = 12	6 x 9 = 54	4 x 8 = 32	6 x 7 = 42	5 x 5 = 25
0 x10 = 0	6 x 1 = 6	5 x 5 = 25	6 x 6 = 36	0 x 2 = 0	7 x 4 = 28	3 x 3 = 9	7 x 9 = 63	6 x 8 = 48	7 x 7 = 49
2 x10 = 20	6 x10 = 60	7 x 1 = 7	9 x 9 = 81	0 x 0 = 0	6 x 2 = 12	8 x 4 = 32	2 x 3 = 6	8 x 9 = 72	9 x 8 = 72
5 x10 = 50	7 x10 = 70	9 x10 = 90	8 x 1 = 8	4 x 4 = 16	5 x 5 = 25	7 x 2 = 14	6 x 4 = 24	1 x 3 = 3	9 x 9 = 81

10's 0's 0's 1's 2's 6's 5's 7's 8's

10's 10's 10's 1's Doubles 2's 4's 3's 9's

Basic Multiplication, Page 10.

4 x 5 = 20	3 x 2 = 6	2 x 6 = 12	1 x 6 = 6	0 x 8 = 0	0's
5 x 6 = 30	4 x 4 = 16	3 x 9 = 27	2 x 7 = 14	1 x 5 = 5	1's
6 x 1 = 6	5 x 7 = 35	4 x 3 = 12	3 x 8 = 24	2 x 8 = 16	2's
7 x 3 = 21	6 x 2 = 12	5 x 8 = 40	4 x 2 = 8	3 x 7 = 21	3's
8 x 8 = 64	7 x 4 = 28	6 x 3 = 18	5 x 9 = 45	4 x 1 = 4	4's
9 x 9 = 81	8 x 9 = 72	7 x 5 = 35	6 x 4 = 24	5 x 5 = 25	5's
10 x 1 = 10	9 x 8 = 72	8 x 1 = 8	7 x 6 = 42	6 x 5 = 30	6's
9 x 5 = 45	10 x 3 = 30	9 x 6 = 54	8 x 2 = 16	7 x 7 = 49	7's
8 x 4 = 32	9 x 9 = 81	10 x 2 = 20	9 x 4 = 36	8 x 3 = 24	8's
10 x 6 = 60	8 x 9 = 72	9 x 8 = 72	10 x 5 = 50	9 x 2 = 18	9's
9 x 9 = 81	10 x 7 = 70	8 x 8 = 64	9 x 1 = 9	10 x 4 = 40	10's
8 x 4 = 32	9 x 7 = 63	10 x 8 = 80	8 x 6 = 48	9 x 5 = 45	9's
7 x 7 = 49	8 x 5 = 40	9 x 5 = 45	10 x 9 = 90	8 x 2 = 16	8's
6 x 6 = 36	7 x 8 = 56	8 x 6 = 48	9 x 3 = 27	10 x 10 = 100	10's
5 x 5 = 25	6 x 9 = 54	7 x 9 = 63	8 x 7 = 56	9 x 1 = 9	9's
4 x 6 = 24	5 x 4 = 20	6 x 8 = 48	7 x 1 = 7	8 x 8 = 64	8's
3 x 3 = 9	4 x 6 = 24	5 x 3 = 15	6 x 7 = 42	7 x 2 = 14	7's
2 x 6 = 12	3 x 4 = 12	4 x 8 = 32	5 x 2 = 10	6 x 6 = 36	6's
1 x 3 = 3	2 x 3 = 6	3 x 5 = 15	4 x 9 = 36	5 x 1 = 5	5's
0 x 6 = 0	1 x 4 = 4	2 x 9 = 18	3 x 9 = 27	4 x 5 = 20	

0's 1's 2's 3's 4's

Basic Multiplication, Page 11.

9 x 3 = 27	[1] x 9 = 9	8 x [8] = 64	9 x 7 = 63	[3] x 5 = 15	7 x [1] = 7	8 x 2 = 16	[2] x 1 = 2	5 x [0] = 0	8 x 0 = 0
[3] x 4 = 12	8 x [3] = 24	2 x 9 = 18	[0] x 8 = 0	3 x [7] = 21	7 x 5 = 35	[3] x 6 = 18	7 x [2] = 14	5 x 1 = 5	any number x 0 = 0
9 x [2] = 18	5 x 4 = 20	[7] x 3 = 21	3 x [9] = 27	3 x 8 = 24	[8] x 7 = 56	9 x [5] = 45	5 x 6 = 30	[6] x 2 = 12	4 x [1] = 4
2 x 2 = 4	[4] x 2 = 8	2 x [4] = 8	6 x 3 = 18	[4] x 9 = 36	7 x [8] = 56	4 x 7 = 28	[4] x 5 = 20	8 x [6] = 48	9 x 2 = 18
[8] x 8 = 64	3 x [3] = 9	8 x 2 = 16	[4] x 4 = 16	5 x [3] = 15	5 x 9 = 45	[4] x 8 = 32	5 x [7] = 35	8 x 5 = 40	[4] x 6 = 24
9 x [1] = 9	1 x 1 = 1	[7] x 7 = 49	3 x [2] = 6	9 x 4 = 36	[4] x 3 = 12	6 x [9] = 54	4 x 8 = 32	[6] x 7 = 42	4 x [6] = 24
0 x 10 = 0	[6] x 1 = 6	5 x [5] = 25	6 x 6 = 36	[0] x 2 = 0	7 x [4] = 28	3 x 3 = 9	[7] x 9 = 63	6 x [8] = 48	7 x 7 = 49
[2] x 10 = 20	6 x [10] = 60	7 x 1 = 7	[9] x 9 = 81	0 x [0] = 0	6 x 2 = 12	[8] x 4 = 32	2 x [3] = 6	8 x 9 = 72	[9] x 8 = 72

Basic Multiplication, Page 12.

5 x 6 = 30	[4] x 4 = 16	3 x [9] = 27	2 x 7 = 14	[1] x 5 = 5
6 x [1] = 6	5 x 7 = 35	[4] x 3 = 12	3 x [6] = 18	2 x 8 = 16
[7] x 3 = 21	6 x [2] = 12	5 x 8 = 40	[5] x 2 = 10	3 x [7] = 21
8 x 8 = 64	[4] x 4 = 16	6 x [3] = 18	5 x 9 = 45	[4] x 1 = 4
9 x [9] = 81	8 x 9 = 72	[7] x 5 = 35	6 x [4] = 24	5 x 5 = 25
[10] x 1 = 10	9 x [8] = 72	8 x 1 = 8	[7] x 6 = 42	6 x [5] = 30
9 x 5 = 45	[10] x 3 = 30	9 x [6] = 54	8 x 2 = 16	[7] x 7 = 49
8 x [4] = 32	9 x 9 = 81	[10] x 2 = 20	9 x [4] = 36	8 x 3 = 24
[10] x 6 = 60	8 x [9] = 72	9 x 8 = 72	[10] x 5 = 50	9 x [2] = 18
9 x 9 = 81	[10] x 7 = 70	8 x [8] = 64	9 x 1 = 9	[10] x 4 = 40
8 x [4] = 32	9 x 7 = 63	[10] x 8 = 80	8 x [6] = 48	9 x 5 = 45
[7] x 7 = 49	8 x [5] = 40	9 x 5 = 45	[10] x 9 = 90	8 x [2] = 16
6 x 6 = 36	[7] x 8 = 56	8 x [7] = 56	9 x 3 = 27	[10] x 10 = 100
5 x [5] = 25	6 x 9 = 54	[7] x 9 = 63	8 x [7] = 56	9 x 1 = 9
[7] x 6 = 42	5 x [4] = 20	6 x 8 = 48	[7] x 1 = 7	8 x [8] = 64
3 x 3 = 9	[4] x 6 = 24	5 x [3] = 15	6 x 7 = 42	[7] x 2 = 14
5 x [6] = 30	3 x 4 = 12	[4] x 8 = 32	5 x [2] = 10	6 x 6 = 36

Basic Division, Page 13.

9)18 = 2	8)16 = 2	7)7 = 1	6)60 = 10	5)20 = 4	4)16 = 4	5)5 = 1	6)18 = 3	7)28 = 4	10)100 = 10	10's
3)12 = 4	9)54 = 6	8)48 = 6	7)35 = 5	6)12 = 2	5)30 = 6	4)28 = 7	5)10 = 2	6)36 = 6	7)21 = 3	7's
4)8 = 2	3)3 = 1	9)72 = 8	8)72 = 9	7)14 = 2	6)54 = 9	5)45 = 9	4)20 = 5	5)50 = 10	6)48 = 8	6's
2)6 = 3	4)12 = 3	3)9 = 3	9)27 = 3	8)64 = 8	7)63 = 9	6)30 = 5	5)15 = 3	4)36 = 9	5)40 = 8	5's
1)3 = 3	2)4 = 2	4)40 = 10	3)30 = 10	9)81 = 9	8)32 = 4	7)70 = 10	6)48 = 8	5)35 = 7	4)24 = 6	4's
3)27 = 9	1)4 = 4	2)2 = 1	4)32 = 8	3)15 = 5	9)36 = 4	8)0 = 0	7)42 = 6	6)24 = 4	5)10 = 2	5's
8)8 = 1	3)18 = 6	1)7 = 7	2)8 = 4	4)12 = 3	3)27 = 9	9)18 = 2	8)40 = 5	7)56 = 8	6)42 = 7	6's
2)18 = 9	8)56 = 7	3)30 = 10	1)5 = 5	2)10 = 5	4)36 = 9	3)18 = 6	9)9 = 1	8)80 = 10	7)49 = 7	7's
10)60 = 6	2)20 = 10	8)72 = 9	3)21 = 7	1)6 = 6	2)16 = 8	4)24 = 6	3)21 = 7	9)18 = 2	8)24 = 3	8's
10)80 = 8	10)30 = 3	2)0 = 0	8)48 = 6	3)0 = 0	1)8 = 8	2)12 = 6	4)28 = 7	3)9 = 3	9)90 = 10	
10's	10's	2's	8's	3's	1's	2's	4's	3's	9's	

Basic Division, Page 14.

4 ÷ 4 = 1	12 ÷ 3 = 4	6 ÷ 2 = 3	6 ÷ 1 = 6	8 ÷ 1 = 8	1's
25 ÷ 5 = 5	8 ÷ 4 = 2	9 ÷ 3 = 3	4 ÷ 2 = 2	5 ÷ 1 = 5	1's
30 ÷ 6 = 5	30 ÷ 5 = 6	16 ÷ 4 = 4	6 ÷ 3 = 2	2 ÷ 2 = 1	2's
0 ÷ 7 = 0	24 ÷ 6 = 4	35 ÷ 5 = 7	12 ÷ 4 = 3	27 ÷ 3 = 9	3's
32 ÷ 8 = 4	7 ÷ 7 = 1	18 ÷ 6 = 3	40 ÷ 5 = 8	20 ÷ 4 = 5	4's
45 ÷ 9 = 5	40 ÷ 8 = 5	14 ÷ 7 = 2	12 ÷ 6 = 2	45 ÷ 5 = 9	5's
80 ÷ 10 = 8	36 ÷ 9 = 4	24 ÷ 8 = 3	21 ÷ 7 = 3	6 ÷ 6 = 1	6's
81 ÷ 9 = 9	100 ÷ 10 = 10	9 ÷ 9 = 1	16 ÷ 8 = 2	28 ÷ 7 = 4	7's
72 ÷ 8 = 9	90 ÷ 9 = 10	60 ÷ 10 = 6	18 ÷ 9 = 2	8 ÷ 8 = 1	8's
63 ÷ 7 = 9	8 ÷ 8 = 1	63 ÷ 9 = 7	40 ÷ 10 = 4	27 ÷ 9 = 3	9's
36 ÷ 6 = 6	56 ÷ 7 = 8	56 ÷ 8 = 7	72 ÷ 9 = 8	20 ÷ 10 = 2	10's
20 ÷ 5 = 4	42 ÷ 6 = 7	49 ÷ 7 = 7	64 ÷ 8 = 8	54 ÷ 9 = 6	9's
28 ÷ 4 = 7	15 ÷ 5 = 3	48 ÷ 6 = 8	42 ÷ 7 = 6	48 ÷ 8 = 6	8's
12 ÷ 3 = 4	36 ÷ 4 = 9	10 ÷ 5 = 2	54 ÷ 6 = 9	35 ÷ 7 = 5	7's
24 ÷ 4 = 6	15 ÷ 3 = 5	32 ÷ 4 = 8	50 ÷ 5 = 10	36 ÷ 6 = 6	6's
45 ÷ 5 = 9	28 ÷ 4 = 7	18 ÷ 3 = 6	28 ÷ 4 = 7	0 ÷ 5 = 0	5''s
60 ÷ 6 = 10	5 ÷ 5 = 1	32 ÷ 4 = 8	21 ÷ 3 = 7	24 ÷ 4 = 6	4''s
6 ÷ 1 = 6	42 ÷ 6 = 7	0 ÷ 5 = 0	40 ÷ 4 = 10	24 ÷ 3 = 8	3's
20 ÷ 2 = 10	2 ÷ 1 = 2	18 ÷ 6 = 3	50 ÷ 5 = 10	36 ÷ 4 = 9	4's
18 ÷ 2 = 9	0 ÷ 2 = 0	10 ÷ 1 = 10	30 ÷ 6 = 5	35 ÷ 5 = 7	
2's	2's	1's	6's	5's	

Basic Division, Page 15.

3)12 = 4	[9])54 = 6	8)[48] = 6	7)35 = 5	[6])12 = 2	5)[30] = 6	4)28 = 7	[5])10 = 2	6)[36] = 6	7)21 = 3
[4])8 = 2	3)[3] = 1	9)72 = 8	[8])72 = 9	7)[14] = 2	6)54 = 9	[5])45 = 9	4)[20] = 5	5)50 = 10	[6])48 = 8
2)[6] = 3	4)12 = 3	[3])9 = 3	9)[81] = 9	8)64 = 8	[7])63 = 9	6)[30] = 5	5)15 = 3	[4])36 = 9	5)[40] = 8
1)3 = 3	[2])4 = 2	4)[40] = 10	3)30 = 10	[9])81 = 9	8)[32] = 4	7)70 = 10	[6])48 = 8	5)[35] = 7	4)24 = 6
[3])27 = 9	1)[4] = 4	2)2 = 1	[4])32 = 8	3)[15] = 5	9)36 = 4	[ ])0 = 0 (any number)	7)[42] = 6	6)24 = 4	[5])10 = 2
8)[8] = 1	3)18 = 6	[1])7 = 7	2)[8] = 4	4)12 = 3	[3])27 = 9	9)[18] = 2	8)40 = 5	[7])56 = 8	6)[42] = 7
2)18 = 9	[8])56 = 7	3)[30] = 10	1)5 = 5	[2])10 = 5	4)[36] = 9	3)18 = 6	[9])9 = 1	8)[80] = 10	7)49 = 7
[10])60 = 6	2)[20] = 10	8)72 = 9	[3])21 = 7	1)[6] = 6	2)16 = 8	[4])24 = 6	3)[21] = 7	9)18 = 2	[8])24 = 3

Basic Division, Page 16.

25 ÷ 5 = 5	[8] ÷ 4 = 2	9 ÷ [3] = 3	4 ÷ 2 = 2	[5] ÷ 1 = 5
30 ÷ [6] = 5	30 ÷ 5 = 6	[16] ÷ 4 = 4	6 ÷ [3] = 2	2 ÷ 2 = 1
[any number] ÷ 0 = 0	24 ÷ [6] = 4	35 ÷ 5 = 7	[12] ÷ 4 = 3	27 ÷ [3] = 9
32 ÷ 8 = 4	[7] ÷ 7 = 1	18 ÷ [6] = 3	40 ÷ 5 = 8	[20] ÷ 4 = 5
45 ÷ [9] = 5	40 ÷ 8 = 5	[14] ÷ 7 = 2	12 ÷ [6] = 2	45 ÷ 5 = 9
[80] ÷ 10 = 8	36 ÷ [9] = 4	24 ÷ 8 = 3	[21] ÷ 7 = 3	6 ÷ [6] = 1
81 ÷ 9 = 9	[100] ÷ 10 = 10	9 ÷ [9] = 1	16 ÷ 8 = 2	[28] ÷ 7 = 4
72 ÷ [8] = 9	90 ÷ 9 = 10	[60] ÷ 10 = 6	18 ÷ [9] = 2	8 ÷ 8 = 1
[63] ÷ 7 = 9	8 ÷ [8] = 1	63 ÷ 9 = 7	[40] ÷ 10 = 4	27 ÷ [9] = 3
36 ÷ 6 = 6	[56] ÷ 7 = 8	56 ÷ [8] = 7	72 ÷ 9 = 8	[20] ÷ 10 = 2
20 ÷ [5] = 4	42 ÷ 6 = 7	[49] ÷ 7 = 7	64 ÷ [8] = 8	54 ÷ 9 = 6
[28] ÷ 4 = 7	15 ÷ [5] = 3	48 ÷ 6 = 8	[42] ÷ 7 = 6	48 ÷ [8] = 6
12 ÷ 3 = 4	[32] ÷ 4 = 8	10 ÷ [5] = 2	54 ÷ 6 = 9	[35] ÷ 7 = 5
24 ÷ [4] = 6	15 ÷ 3 = 5	[16] ÷ 4 = 4	50 ÷ [10] = 5	36 ÷ 6 = 6
[45] ÷ 5 = 9	28 ÷ [4] = 7	18 ÷ 3 = 6	[28] ÷ 4 = 7	40 ÷ [5] = 8
45 ÷ 9 = 5	[5] ÷ 5 = 1	32 ÷ [4] = 8	21 ÷ 3 = 7	[24] ÷ 4 = 6
6 ÷ [1] = 6	60 ÷ 10 = 6	[0] ÷ 5 = 0	40 ÷ [8] = 5	24 ÷ 3 = 8

Advanced Addition, Page 17.

13 + 45 = 58	32 + 37 = 69	15 + 24 = 39	44 + 14 = 58	23 + 72 = 95	21 + 22 + 23 = 66	35 + 23 + 11 = 69	2 digits columns no regrouping
513 + 64 = 577	24 + 603 = 627	323 + 56 = 379	832 + 32 = 864	417 + 40 + 31 = 488	744 + 32 + 10 = 786	525 + 52 + 11 = 588	2 digits + 3 digits columns no regrouping
36 + 29 = 65	27 + 34 = 61	57 + 23 = 80	73 + 18 = 91	26 + 86 = 112	49 + 65 = 114	98 + 88 = 186	2 digits + 2 digits regrouping
46 + 26 + 16 = 88	19 + 50 + 28 = 97	53 + 28 + 15 = 96	41 + 16 + 27 = 84	67 + 66 + 65 = 198	85 + 95 + 55 = 235	93 + 94 + 95 = 282	2 digits columns regrouping
324 + 36 = 360	627 + 47 = 674	866 + 25 = 891	294 + 576 = 870	368 + 347 = 715	298 + 304 = 602		2/3 digits + 3 digits regrouping
769 + 754 = 1,523	381 + 709 = 1,090	576 + 557 = 1,133	274 + 790 = 1,064	894 + 858 = 1,752	631 + 769 = 1,400		3 digits + 3 digits regrouping
1,492 + 1,986 = 3,478	4,455 + 7,786 = 12,241	42,791 + 23,489 = 66,280	487,692 + 255,508 = 743,200	2,987,465 + 8,978,645 = 11,966,110			multiple digits regrouping

Advanced Addition, Page 18.

4 + 4 + 1 = 9	2 + **6** + 2 = 10	6 + 0 + **3** = 9	1 + 2 + 5 = 8	**5** + 7 + 2 = 14	8 + **3** + 6 = 17	4 + 9 + **6** = 19
52 + **24** = 76	**11** + 82 = 93	56 + 43 = 99	70 + **19** = 89	**24** + 24 = 48	**23** + 11 + 33 = 67	35 + **23** + 11 = 69
417 + 72 = 489	513 + **64** = 577	942 + 30 = 972	**417** + 40 + 31 = 488	523 + **23** + 23 = 569	713 + 46 + 30 = 789	224 + 132 + **111** = 467
35 + 7 = 42	88 + 2 = 90	28 + **9** = 37	**44** + 8 = 52	47 + 6 = 53	**19** + 27 = 46	18 + **25** = 43
68 + 54 = 122	**94** + 96 = 190	64 + **36** = 100	46 + 85 = 131	**47** + 28 + 15 = 90	19 + **28** + 18 = 65	18 + 64 + 69 = 151
440 + 39 = 479	278 + **19** = 297	**509** + 99 = 608	594 + 186 = 780	394 + **575** = 969	**386** + 239 = 625	472 + 668 = 1,140
2,468 + 1,912 = 4,380	1,327 + 9,857 = 11,184	28,097 + **11,646** = 39,743	**5,547,606** + 7,568,705 = 13,116,311			

Advanced Subtraction, Page 19.

89 - 52 = 37	167 - 37 = 130	882 - 631 = 251	795 - 33 = 762	987 - 456 = 531	768 - 432 = 336	2/3 digits - 2/3 digits no regrouping
98 - 49 = 49	51 - 34 = 17	92 - 28 = 64	82 - 56 = 26	75 - 28 = 47	73 - 26 = 47	2 digits - 2 digits regrouping
765 - 18 = 747	977 - 29 = 948	372 - 67 = 305	748 - 567 = 181	936 - 284 = 652	814 - 373 = 441	3 digits - 2/3 digits regrouping
357 - 199 = 158	621 - 149 = 472	971 - 565 = 406	872 - 186 = 686	523 - 147 = 376	743 - 265 = 478	3 digits - 3 digits regrouping
700 - 524 = 176	801 - 137 = 664	670 - 485 = 185	900 - 462 = 438	509 - 269 = 240	403 - 148 = 255	zero concept regrouping
64,005 - 21,564 = 42,441	9,786 - 8,898 = 888	27,142 - 16,193 = 10,949	87,942 - 28,853 = 59,089			multiple digits

Advanced Subtraction, Page 20.

77 - 3 = 74	89 - **6** = 83	68 - 22 = 46	**29** - 9 = 20	36 - **14** = 22	97 - 43 = 54
24 - 5 = 19	**42** - 8 = 34	80 - **36** = 44	51 - 8 = 43	**56** - 18 = 38	72 - **68** = 4
883 - **30** = 853	**747** - 24 = 723	882 - 631 = 251	**165** - 56 = 109	276 - **38** = 238	493 - 27 = 466
674 - 146 = 528	813 - **459** = 354	**435** - 247 = 188	644 - 176 = 468	657 - **268** = 389	**916** - 548 = 368
800 - **564** = 236	**910** - 351 = 559	407 - 239 = 168	500 - **155** = 345	**820** - 276 = 544	704 - 306 = 398
4,276 - 357 = 3,919	7,842 - **1,986** = 5,856	56,235 - 24,891 = 31,344	**84,531** - 65,974 = 18,557		

Advanced Multiplication, Page 21.

56 x 5 = 280	70 x 6 = 420	49 x 9 = 441	64 x 8 = 512	39 x 7 = 273	2 digits x 1 digit
492 x 4 = 1,968	300 x 5 = 1,500	628 x 6 = 3,768	749 x 9 = 6,741	508 x 8 = 4,064	3 digits x 1 digit
436 x 58 = 25,288	257 x 40 = 10,280	587 x 39 = 22,893	823 x 75 = 61,725	784 x 96 = 75,264	2 digits x 3 digits
456 x 329 = 150,024	357 x 400 = 142,800	706 x 405 = 285,930	376 x 284 = 106,784	592 x 438 = 259,296	3 digits x 3 digits zero concept
995 x 897 = 892,515	9,000 x 800 = 7,200,000	4,873 x 95 = 462,935	5,870 x 674 = 3,956,380	2,478 x 352 = 872,256	mutliple digits zero concept

Advanced Multiplication, Page 22.

32 x 4 = 128	51 x **3** = 153	74 x 2 = 148	**83** x 3 = 249	90 x **8** = 720
93 x 5 = 465	**77** x 4 = 308	58 x **6** = 348	68 x 9 = 612	**76** x 5 = 380
407 x 6 = 2,442	568 x **2** = 1,136	533 x 3 = 1,599	**628** x 9 = 5,652	671 x **8** = 5,368
14 x 15 = 210	**47** x 28 = 1,316	74 x **36** = 2,664	57 x 85 = 4,845	**98** x 40 = 3,920
345 x 62 = 21,390	298 x **25** = 7,450	607 x 47 = 28,529	**300** x 500 = 150,000	294 x **256** = 75,264
417 x 383 = 159,711	264 x 804 = 212,256	**5,407** x 42 = 227,094	2,894 x **186** = 538,284	

Advanced Division, Page 23.

5)38 = 7 R3	6)27 = 4 R3	3)81 = 27	4)84 = 21	5)90 = 18	2 digits ÷ 1 digit
6)76 = 12 R4	5)94 = 18 R4	8)891 = 111 R3	7)882 = 126	4)915 = 228 R3	2/3 digits ÷ 1 digit
29)87 = 3	16)93 = 5 R13	30)810 = 27	42)970 = 23 R4	92)999 = 10 R79	2/3 digits ÷ 2 digits
37)8,658 = 234	83)9,960 = 120	39)6,000 = 153 R33	48)46,261 = 963 R37	72)89,496 = 1243	4/5 digits ÷ 2 digits
250)95,500 = 382	701)64,549 = 92 R57	342)712,044 = 2082	692)641,950 = 927 R466	547)896,721 = 1639 R188	multiple digits ÷ 3 digits

Advanced Division, Page 24.

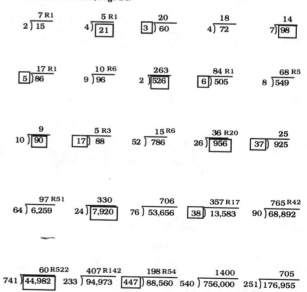

2)15 = 7 R1	4)**21** = 5 R1	**3**)60 = 20	4)72 = 18	7)**98** = 14
5)86 = 17 R1	9)96 = 10 R6	2)**526** = 263	**6**)505 = 84 R1	8)549 = 68 R5
10)**90** = 9	**17**)88 = 5 R3	52)786 = 15 R6	26)**956** = 36 R20	**37**)925 = 25
64)6,259 = 97 R51	24)**7,920** = 330	76)53,656 = 706	**38**)13,583 = 357 R17	90)68,892 = 765 R42
741)**44,982** = 60 R522	233)94,973 = 407 R142	**447**)88,560 = 198 R54	540)756,000 = 1400	251)176,955 = 705

Assessment Test, Page 25.

21 + 4 25	12 + 7 19	32 + 6 38	18 + 1 19	62 + 5 67	41 + 7 48	36 + 3 39	2 digits + 1 digit no regrouping
23 + 8 31	54 + 6 60	29 + 7 36	16 + 9 25	32 + 8 40	88 + 6 94	79 + 5 84	2 digits + 1 digit regrouping
43 + 87 130	59 + 46 105	73 + 98 171	77 + 35 112	94 + 29 123	76 + 45 121	89 + 88 177	2 digits + 2 digits regrouping
13 29 + 17 59	27 28 + 14 69	36 23 + 29 88	24 18 + 17 59	77 77 + 77 231	56 46 + 48 150	98 94 + 19 211	columns regrouping
132 + 48 180	118 + 34 152	207 + 64 271	655 + 66 721	247 + 75 322	534 + 86 620		3 digits + 2 digits regrouping
359 + 578 937	285 + 539 824	174 + 508 682	689 + 734 1,423	483 + 838 1,321	545 + 669 1,214		3 digits + 3 digits regrouping
6,719 + 1,299 8,018	132,074 + 678,349 810,423	237,601 + 948,709 1,186,310	827,621 + 746,587 1,574,208	987,465 + 978,645 1,966,110			multiple digits regrouping

Assessment Test, Page 26.

24 - 5 19	30 - 6 24	42 - 8 34	31 - 4 27	62 - 8 54	43 - 7 36	86 - 9 77	2 dig 1 dig regro
90 - 24 66	51 - 15 36	98 - 49 49	52 - 27 25	92 - 39 53	61 - 43 18	85 - 26 59	2 dig 2 dig regr
638 - 48 590	522 - 97 425	345 - 56 289	782 - 91 691	276 - 87 189	333 - 82 251		3 dig 2 dig regr
250 - 125 125	381 - 292 89	354 - 117 237	836 - 268 568	910 - 285 625	427 - 208 219		3 dig 3 dig regr
420 - 115 305	807 - 174 633	870 - 326 544	608 - 399 209	906 - 207 699	700 - 234 466		zero regr
6,002 - 2,453 3,549	7,342 - 1,565 5,777	15,167 - 12,368 2,799	86,723 - 47,268 39,455	86,271 - 79,452 6,819			mult digit regro

Assessment Test, Page 27.

63 x 7 441	75 x 6 450	39 x 9 351	59 x 4 236	48 x 5 240	2 digits x 1 digit
678 x 56 37,968	243 x 27 6,561	493 x 83 40,919	389 x 89 34,621	642 x 65 41,730	3 digits x 2 digits
213 x 124 26,412	397 x 486 192,942	258 x 274 70,692	998 x 989 987,022	548 x 813 445,524	3 digits x 3 digits
100 x 57 5,700	949 x 70 66,430	700 x 700 490,000	405 x 90 36,450	564 x 800 451,200	zero concept
4,673 x 53 247,699	5,407 x 42 227,094	2,894 x 186 538,284	6,677 x 549 3,665,673	4,927 x 238 1,172,626	multiple digits

Assessment Test, Page 28.

5 R4 5) 29	5 R1 2) 11	8 R2 7) 58	8 R2 8) 66	10 9) 90	2 dig 1 di
15 R3 4) 63	9 R1 3) 28	139 R2 7) 975	216 R3 4) 867	139 R4 6) 838	2/3 1 di
5 12) 60	4 R12 21) 96	52 18) 936	23 R10 30) 700	23 R4 42) 970	2/3 2 di
45 50) 2,250	84 29) 2,436	2674 R14 34) 90,930	238 R4 42) 10,000		4/5 2 di
150 R78 308) 46,278	179 R338 478) 85,900	536 187) 100,232	1400 540) 756,000		5/6 3 di